The Battle of Lola Mayne

R.D. RENTMEESTER

Published by Fallblind Industries

Copyright © 2020 R.D. Rentmeester

The moral right of the author has been asserted.

Cover Design by R.D. Rentmeester
Typeset and arranged by Up & Up Media

First published 2020

First Edition
9780648493853

All rights reserved.

This book is sold subject to the condition that it shall not be lent, hired out, or circulated in any form of binding or cover other than that in which it is published.

No part of this work may be reproduced, stored in a retrieval system, or transmitted in any form or by any means (electronic, mechanical, photocopying, recording, or otherwise) without the prior written permission of Fallblind Industries, except in the case of brief quotations embodied in critical articles and reviews.

The views expressed in this works do not necessarily reflect the views of the publisher or author.

Printed Locally: Australia, USA, UK

Since the first glance;

Sunbeams encapsulating tiny universes seamlessly dancing across your face in the corner of a West End coffee shop.

The flicking of your yellow coated HB pencil as you drew eyes so beautiful they could almost compete with your own; stopping briefly, ever so often, to raise the eraser to your tender, unblemished lips, before lowering your artistic sword back into your unmatchable brilliance.

Nervously I approached.
'I'm sorry,' I disrupt, almost at a whisper, as not to alarm. 'I saw you from across the room and felt compelled to introduce myself,' I continued meekly.
Coy.
Disarmed.
She smiled gracefully, raising her gaze to meet mine.
Two crystal blue pools of radiant perfection shimmering back toward me.

'Hello... My name is Lola...'

The Battle of
Lola Mayne

'Je t'ai dans la peau…'

CHAPTER ONE
INFATUATION

INFATUATION

Waking up from this dream.
I walk down to the corner shop,
I catch alight and then I think of you.
Reflections caught in the breeze.

Everywhere that I've been.
I see your face on every face,
Your scent in every sense of all that means.
Where nothing's quite as it seems.

Tried my best to stay clean.
But a shadow moves and I feel your flame,
That same old fire deep inside my veins.
Where your smile drives me insane.

The tide of seas rearranged.
The waves all crash,
On shores of self,
It won't be long until you are here with me.
Just waking up from this dream.

The battle's just begun.
And we are right where we belong.
To all the wars we've left behind.
I am yours and you are mine.

It was hard to distinguish whether her waves came through like the curling waters of a crystal blue ocean at high tide, or more so of the static noise rupturing from an old broken television set, but either way I could feel her with me constantly.
Laced through every dream, every thought.
A silk layer cast across every bleeding emotion.
A rabbit trap grip upon my entirety.

She was there.

I recall pondering whether or not Lola's thoughts reflected my own.

Sticking to 'the old boys' code' I had waited two days to call the number Lola had written to me on an old matchbook she had in her handbag.

Flicking the matchbook around my pocket, I decided there was no time like the present, and typed the numbers into my phone.

THE BATTLE OF LOLA MAYNE

Deep within the shadows of my own personal requiem,
She pushes me up against the wall,
And sucker-punches her lips to mine.
My knuckles turn white as I claw with certainty to keep a grip on this dream.
'We're in this together now,' she whispers,
Her warm breath swirling at my lobe as my eyelids roll upward.
Enchanted,
I awake.

INFATUATION

The suffering made me strong.
Hardened the shell.
Prepared me for battle.
The colour of my skin is irrelevant,
as my blood still pumps scarlet.
These lips still breathe fire.
Let them underestimate the power of one.
And as the illusive world that they have constructed around them burns to the ground,
Cinders to ash,
They will repent.
They will know my name.

We were standing at a bar in old Chinatown midway through our first date. At the time, I had a grunge lustre for ripped jeans and checkered shirts, whereas Lola's style was far more graceful. Dainty even. I could feel every eye in the room side-glancing us, questioning our affiliation.

A guy approached from the other side of the room, standing between us with his back toward me.

'So, is this your brother?'

'My brother?' Lola laughed. 'No sir, this is my fiancé,' she smiled, condescendingly patting him on the shoulder.

'Well where is your ring then?' he sneered in retaliation, pointing toward her hand.

Lola's smile shifted briefly.

'I don't think that's any of your business, sir; now off you go.' She spoke firmly, tilting her head to the side to suggest his exit route.

He walked away. We continued our date.

INFATUATION

One man walks,
While another man crawls.
While another man tries to slide up the wall.
One man waits,
While another escapes.
This man came for you.
One man's climb,
Is another man's fall.
One man's time,
Isn't about time at all.
One man's reach,
Is another man's speech.
This man came for you.
One man triumphs,
In the middle of a street.
One man fails,
While the other man repeats.
One man is lost,
While another man is found.
This man came for you.

She lit up my life with the brilliant light of a field filled with fireflies.
The moon beaming atop crops of gold riddled passion.
A collision of two universes unfurled for the world to see.
A killing spree of my every defence.
Her skin was the atmospheric limitation to a world I longed to dive into.
A soul filled with a hazy mist flooded in hurricanes of shooting stars and dynamite.
All of her intricate details shone like the first sun.
All of her soul awakening aspirations lay comfort as I fell harder than I ever had before.

I burnt brighter around her.

INFATUATION

I would proclaim your absolute beauty to the entire world.
Build statues in your honour,
and avenge all of your sorrows.
I would plant fields full of the
brightest flowers for you to lay upon;
And clear clouds from the sky so the stars can watch you shine.
I would move mountains,
build cities,
And dig up tombs of pharaohs.
There isn't a single thing I would not do for you.
As you,
my goddess,
are as important as the final tear that trickled from Christ's weary eye;
Laced with the blood from the thorny crown above.
Biblical.
Symbolic.
But the constellation itself,
although seen a trillion times over,
Is very rarely noticed.
But it is still present.
Still valid.
Still meaningful.
As are you.

THE BATTLE OF LOLA MAYNE

I anticipate the warm touch of your lips upon mine.
Two heavenly bodies, entangled within each other's arms.
Legs flailing in the breeze from atop the twisted branches of an old oak tree.
My fingers in your hair;
Yours, upon my face.
We sit suspended somewhere within the ticks of the clock.
Entrapped, staring into each other's eyes.
Your coy smile speaking volumes.
My hungry eyes reading the pages.

Nobody can touch us here.

INFATUATION

Lola and I were debating whether or not Van Gogh actually cared for the socioeconomics of the people which he had painted and things were getting heated. Her passion for art had ignited something inside of me as she stood, hand in an outward fashion, affirming the point she was trying to deliver.

Without any warning, I pressed my lips against hers.

Lola paused for a second. Surprised, before pushing her lips back to mine. Within debate, our first kiss manifested.

THE BATTLE OF LOLA MAYNE

Soul binding;
With undertones of menacing enchantment.
Two quarter moons eclipsing across the amber aura of a fading summer sky.
A transfixing silhouette of beauty,
undeniably unmatchable.
And atop the shadow of beaming rainbows,
I watch the colours explode as she passes them by.
I have built empires in my head.
Where I am the king,
And she is my queen.
They worship our union,
for there is no other like it.

This universe is hers.

INFATUATION

Give me your heart,
and I will capture all of the stars in the sky to protect it.
Show me your mind,
and I will swim within it like the crystal blue waters off a Costa Rican shore.
Show me your soul,
and I will blur deep within the resonating light it shines.
Because although unique,
my job here is simple.
Just a vessel sent from the gods above to remind you of your utmost importance and delicate beauty within the world around you.
You carry the light of the stars and the depths of the sea,
the tune of precisely strung orchestras in the greatest of halls,
and the scent of man's wildest desires.

I could get locked in your eyes for an eternity.
Floating aimlessly in the distance between us,
like light suspended from the sun upon a flake of dust.
I could spend my whole life delving depths of your universe that no other has yet discovered;
parts of your soul that nobody else has seen.
For it is you that I yearn for.
It is you that I crave.
Within heartbeats and breaths,
your entirety circles around my being;
Forever grateful that I found you when I needed you most.

INFATUATION

I've always found it strange how we only seem to remember the mountainous memories when it comes to 'how we fall in love'. Trips away. Adventures. Mini golf on a brisk Sunday morning. But the real connection usually happens somewhere within those fleeting moments we too often take for granted. Wrestling on the bed. Sharing thoughts and ideologies unto one another within the warm confinements of a voluptuous sofa. Debate from across the kitchen table. For this is where the true obscurity of love blossoms.

You are a goddess.
Handcrafted with the light of the sun.
Softened with stardust.
Shaded by moonlight.
All of your intricate pieces,
woven together,
with consuming perfection.
A smile that could end wars.
A look that could create them.

INFATUATION

It's the little things.
Like the distance in her voice when we say goodbye.
Both knowing that each second is going to feel like a millennia
    until we get to hear each other's voice again.
Even the most comfortable of mattresses
or billion thread-count sheets,
could not eliminate the bed of nails we both lay upon,
waiting to see each other again.
Passion infused sentences,
conversations between angels.

Often, Lola would disappear completely for days on end. It took a lot of self growth to conform to this behaviour, especially considering she masked my every thought.

I did, however, need to be somewhat sympathetic to the pressures of an Ivy League art school. She would assure me that it was not that she didn't wish to be near me, she had just worked her ass off to get here, and didn't want anything to jeopardise her studies. I respected her ethic, although difficult to adjust to.

INFATUATION

Close your eyes and I'll speak to you,
everything you want me to.
Make you happy without lies,
tears of joy I'll make you cry.
Without you in my life,
I don't think I'd survive.
Cuddle up now close to me,
because you know I will always be.
Forever and a day,
and I will never change.
As my love grows for you,
I hope that yours does too.
And since the day we met,
I believe that you're heaven sent.
All so sweet and so divine,
I hope you will always be mine.

I.

Need you now.

Here with me.

I take her hand and stare far across the reach of humanity, out toward the horizon.

'If I could give you the world, I would,' I preach to her as her eyes glisten with a smile.

'But you have given me you, and now I have the world,' she responds, melting my heart with captivating intensity.

We look out as the street lights dance systematically with the headlights of the cars passing between them.

Where they are going isn't relevant to me. For my whole universe holds her arm around my side, taking in the same ember fuelled drug as I:

Us.

INFATUATION

The pressure of petals upon your skin.
Much like the delicacy of broken butterfly wings.
Between fingertips.
The jagged edges of the world fade;
If only for a minute.

You are bare.
Vulnerable.
Intoxicated by touch.

The pressure Lola placed upon herself in pursuit of a fulfilling education eventually wore her emotionally thin.

We had just moved into our first apartment together and I vividly recall coming home one afternoon and hearing her tossing brushes, paints and profanities about within her creative space.

I awaited in the hall by the entrance as the commotion whittled to silence.

After a few brief moments, the door lever clicked, followed by the timely squeal of unoiled hinges.

Lola looked up at me, tears dwelling in her eyes.

'My Dali interpretation is terrible, and it's worth a quarter of my final!' she sobbed in the doorway.

'Come with me,' I proposed delicately, reaching my hand out toward hers.

INFATUATION

I lead you to the darkness,
So I can give to you;
What you gave to me.
I wrap my arms around you,
Following it with a kiss;
For the happiness that you bring.
My whole world revolves around you,
I have faith in all that you do.

You make my world complete.

THE BATTLE OF LOLA MAYNE

Hurricanes of unforgettable motion.
Our souls, twisting and curving within one another.
Unchained passion.
Immeasurable heat.
Like a finger caressing the pin of a hand grenade;
Idling on the temptation of when to release.
The entrapment of butterflies,
the sound of oceans.

INFATUATION

And in that moment we were free.
Free to be ourselves.
Free to tear all of our uncertainties and insecurities to shreds.
As we collided like rival war beings across scuffed linen beneath us.
Locks of your hair in my hand,
nail marks carved down my back.
Humidity fogging all twelve windows of our humble domain.
Within this moment,
we were warriors.
Fighting against each other,
for each other.

Lola was different to anyone before her. Our rhythm and intimacy unmatchable. A union of two souls. It was as if I had awoken in the chambers of a forbidden realm, frozen somewhere in the sands of time. Static impulses curling the absolute fibre of our beings and racing unstoppably throughout one another. Sweat atop our flesh. Fire within our veins. The electricity with which our bodies collided was not a feeling I had ever experienced before; nor a feeling I would ever share with anyone else again.

INFATUATION

You came to me as a dream within a dream.
Soft whispers passed through tender lips.
Blinding vision of a love that bleeds,
and burns,
simultaneously.
Untamed passions thrown across the sheets like two lions fighting for the pride.

And until the end of time;

I am yours and you are mine.

The concept of heaven is well and truly alive,

I have seen it.

I have felt it.

Not when I laid lifeless on the rain stricken asphalt.
Nor when my eyes rolled back into my head after a night hit far too hard.
But when I was within your arms.
When I got to gaze into your eyes and feel your warmth surround me.

Sober.

Drug free.

Yet more intoxicated than ever before.

Content.

Collected.

You are how I know the concept of heaven is real.

CHAPTER TWO
ALLIANCE

ALLIANCE

Bring to me our souls entwined,
and let us drink lattes together as we watch the sunshine creep over the distant horizon.
Let me feel your warmth surround me as laughter echoes in our ears from children at play.
Let us not fall into desperation,
seeking each other's truths.
As we already know.
Two souls catapulted into each other,
and without limitation,
we soar.
Electrical impulse neither can deny.
A marrying of magnetic pull and gravitational diligence.
Soul mates.
Soul lovers.
We are,
and will always be,
what they one day wish to be.
But without this connection,
they are sure to get it wrong.

I love you.

I adore you.

No, wait.
I absolutely idolise you.
When you step into the room,
the rest of the world disappears.
As does the sadness,
the emptiness,
and the longing.
The room turns silent.
The people fade.
And it's just us.

Lola shone with the intensity of the most blinding city lights as she stood, diploma in hand, with a countless amount of gleaming eyes upon her.

A secret smile of relief that until this moment I had not seen, as if the jaws of life had finally released her from their vice like grip.

Distinction after distinction, sleepless night after sleepless night, had finally paid their dues. After all of this time, my queen was at the then pinnacle moment of her entire life; and I had never been prouder.

Your eyes.
They drive me crazy.
Your skin.
It feels so warm.
Tonight.
We'll watch the angels.
Come down.
From heaven above.
They watch.
They watch you baby.
You dance.
Like never before.
If you.
Were not my lady.
Then I.
Would rather be alone.

Never say goodbye.

And when you ask me,
'Why do you treat me so special?'
I answer swiftly,
'Because you are special.'
Because your every move makes my heart melt like the candles within an otherwise bleak church beneath the moonlight,
far before the break of the sun.
Because you are made of a billion screaming stars that catapult me into a place where the fire burns brighter.
A place where plagues of butterflies batter at the inside of my heart, making me feel that warm rush of blood to my chest. The godly scent that could rock me to sleep in the loudest storm.
You are special because I can see in you, all of the beautiful things that you cannot see within yourself.
Which ironically,
makes you even more beautiful.

You are the itch I cannot stop scratching,
the wound that will never heal.
The pulse that bleeds life and light into every crack that I bear.
The reason for my breath, and heartbeat.
You are the single most important constellation of cells that I have ever felt.
My appetite craves only you.
You are the rise of the first known sun,
the imbalance in my chemistry.
Without you, I am but flesh.
No heart.
Nor soul.
It is for you I continue.
For you I grit my teeth,
clench my fists,
And bow my head.
For I have not known heaven on earth until your arrival.
And just your presence alone reassures me that there is a god.
My faith is in you,
and nothing else will ever matter as much.

ALLIANCE

When your walls are falling,
when there's nowhere to turn.
Until there's nothing left,
for every single breath;
I'll be there.

And in your darkest hour,
where words don't seem to fit.
Until the end of time,
forever you and I;
I'll be there.

Who would have known it was going to be damn near impossible to obtain work for an overqualified art major? Month upon month of interviews and applications were getting us nowhere and Lola was sick of making glorified coffee for the masses. In her times of trouble, between tears and tantrums, all I could do was try and keep pushing us forward. Teamwork.

ALLIANCE

You have no obligation to me.
All that I ask,
is that you be yourself.
The strong,
independent,
wildfire whom I fell for years ago.
The girl with the melting smile,
and hurricane heart.
I will not confine you to fear invoked limitations.
I would far rather watch you ignite the dreams of your childhood self,
and follow the path as they lead you to who you truly are.
I am not your keeper,
although for you my heart shines.
Partnership.
Not ownership.

THE BATTLE OF LOLA MAYNE

I had no plans to be a renegade,
or a revolutionary within the battlefields of love.
I had no plans of disrupting life as it flowed around me,
as I searched eagerly,
Trying to find a place I could belong.
I had no plans of stumbling into situations that would force me to re-evaluate my judgement and the complexities between right and wrong;
Nor did I plan to find the comfort of home within your eyes.
Before you,
there were no plans.

'Dear Miss Mayne,

We are excited to inform you that your application to curate at the Metropolitan Museum of Art, New York City, New York, has been successful. We admire your credentials and look forward to working alongside you.

Please reply to this email at your greatest convenience.'

And just like that, after years of studying and months of grievous searching, Miss Mayne had started her dream career.

What we made rarely comes as easily as it did us.
A homefront built on foundations of laughter and divine admiration.
A place where truths lie without cautious footings and passions flare within singular breaths.
The dark burden of loneliness negated and in its place, the glimmer of sun rays across pure blue waters.
To my favourite of humans,
my weapon of choice.
The life I value most;
I love you,
in this lifetime,
and the next.

ALLIANCE

There is no piece of my heart that you have not yet consumed.
No particle of my soul that is not yet yours alone.
The fabricated boundaries between what is you,
what is I,
and what is us,
have merged into a muddled realm of obscurity.
Like two soft clays being hard pressed together.
We are one.

When they speak of us,
'A magical universe of their own,' is the only definition that will suffice.

And if your lips pressed against mine are the last that I feel,
then I'll know that I have succeeded in life.
I will continue to trip galaxies on angel wings,
knowing that I have been given all the spoils of life's splendour.

Reminiscing the night we collided;
Like lion and lamb.
Your honey smeared across my lips,
as lust bled from our pores.
I gnawed at your skin,
hands tangled in your hair.
Your sighs fading into the night;
My switchblade tongue.

ALLIANCE

When I speak to you of forever,
I do not mean until the next comes along.
I do not mean until I am disenfranchised in your interests,
or until your face becomes that familiar to me that you seem to blend into the crowd.
Your interests will always fascinate me,
and no other,
no matter how popular,
or beautiful,
or intriguingly complex,
will ever hold a candle to how I feel about you.
When I speak to you of forever,
I mean until death divides us;
And beyond.

Throughout this life,

and far into the next.

I found myself in you.
I found a whole world where
dreams come true.
A fire that never fades.
A torch to light the way.
And with every step closer to you,
I was a step closer to myself.

Atop a broken rail bridge, far from the entombing hustle and stresses of big city culture, Lola and I sat. Legs dangling over the edge, our eyes fixed far into the distance.

I can still vividly recall how nice the sun felt upon my skin, and the radiating glow atop daisies that grew from cracks in the decaying sleepers.

Within the comfort of silence, only quietly shadowed by the relaxing undertones of insects, I reached into my backpack.

Scuffling about, Lola became alerted to my plight.

'What are you looking for?' She laughed at my incapacity to do the simplest of tasks without cosmic interference.

'Marriage?' I suggested nervously, pulling the ring from my satchel, holding it toward her like a child on 'show and tell' day, allowing the diamonds to lure.

'Took your time,' Lola smiled gleefully, allowing me to slide the shiny cuff upon her finger.

THE BATTLE OF LOLA MAYNE

Jailed in your heart.
Drenched in your love.
Each moment more fragile than the next.
Consumed by your soul.
Entombed by your eyes.
An impenetrable glistening atmosphere,
made only for us.
Decoded by your beauty.
Enriched by your words.
Seven-point-eight-billion people in the world;
And all,
I need,
is her.

ALLIANCE

There will be no more queens.
No more tireless efforts to try and replicate something that should never be replaced.
For our union is far more special than the last;
Or the next.
Hand stitched and woven throughout each other's radiance,
our hearts forever beat as one.
At checkpoints, where either could have crumbled;
We instead conjured strength,
and stood taller than the times before.
Together now, we are bulletproof.
Our foundations have been tested far greater than others, but they have never faulted, or cracked.
Instead gaining reinforcement from each test put before them.
It is within these testaments that we must let our light shine brightest.
Protect this unity at all costs.
Breath in the darkness,
And exhale fireflies.

There is no further need for searching.

There will be no more queens.

THE BATTLE OF LOLA MAYNE

When the moon and the stars are shining so bright.
And the steam from your body is consuming the night.
When the air that you breathe gets harder to take.
And the fever inside you is about to escape.

Wherever this emptiness goes.
Whenever the pain has gone.
From here until the end of all time,
it will be you and I.

I will love you.
I will wipe away all of your tears.
You'll never be alone.
Because I will always be here.
I'm your king.
And you are my queen.
We'll never be apart.
Forever and everything.

ALLIANCE

Not bricks, nor mortar,
not tiles, nor stone;
Wherever you are,
is where I call home.

I watched as my best friend, my lover, my soulmate, all rolled into one captivating whole, walked toward me.

A banquet of emotions ricocheting off one another internally, like bullets flying unsystematically through a saloon of an old western film.

Fighting to keep my composure I stood statuesque. Afraid that if I moved a single inch, I would awake from this dream, shattering the beautiful glow around me.

As the footsteps drew nearer down the aisle I could only slightly make out those distinctive, luscious lips that I had fallen for on the day we first met. Before her, the flower girls laid paper white rose petals at her feet as the gold laced silk train slithered behind her.

Upon Lola's arrival, and with permission from the priest, I lifted her veil to reveal the blue oceanic pools that I called home.

Here we stood, hands grasping one another's and tears forming in each of our eyes as the church bells rang thrice.

'We are gathered here today ...'

The answer,
is you.
It always has been you.
It always will be you.
We were destined,
lifetimes ago.
I cannot recall what I was doing before the day we met;
It doesn't seem at all relevant now.
For we are a parable of fate's success.
From the moment my eyes fell intoxicatingly into the depths of yours;
And as I thrashed helplessly in their oceanic pools of magic;
I knew,
I was home.

I am forever grateful.
Forever appreciative.
Forever yours.

I love you.

The starlight of your infinite galaxy awoke me.
Before you, I was floating aimlessly through time and space.
Your existence healed my wounds,
and softened the piercing nails,
bluntened the edges;
And released me from their grip.
There are so many ways I want to repay you,
and show you just how important you are.
From soft whispers in the mornings;
A slow and seductive caress.
To the sound of big bands and mighty trombones.
As I scream my devotion to you from every mountain top.
It is for you that I smile,
and my heart beats strong.
It is for you that my knees go weak,
and butterflies batter their hardy wings around my insides.
It is for you that I breathe,
the mightiest winds of monsoons.
And it is for you,
that I burn,
these infernos.

CHAPTER THREE
FRAGILITY

At first, it was a single gunshot somewhere off in the distance.

A murmur from the other side of an almost empty room.

A single bullet ricocheting off a course brick facade.

A string of carefully thought out words.

Rehearsed, I assume.

A barrage of well planned tyrannies.

A machine gun unapologetically unloading upon an unsuspecting marketplace as the occupants scream and run for cover.

And then came the bombs.

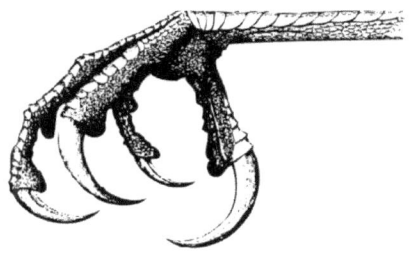

Instead of formulating your retaliation as I speak,
Hear my words.
Listen to them.
Acknowledge them.
As these aren't just my thoughts,
This is how you make me feel.

I remember standing in the kitchen, Lola scowling toward me from across the room as I stood dumbfounded with a frypan in one hand, and a dishcloth in the other.

'All I have done throughout this entire marriage is support you! You tell me to jump, and I fucking jump! What do you want from me?!' I aggressively let the words linger, trampling her like a stampede on the opposing side of the room.

All too familiar with this style of interaction, she shakes her head, the look of disappointment toward our current climate drawn noticeably across her face.

'I just want you to leave me alone,' Lola replies calmly, disarming my aggression before exiting the room.

'How the fuck did we get here?'

THE BATTLE OF LOLA MAYNE

Cold stare, from across this jaded room.
I am right here if you need me.
But if you leave and this darkness consumes you,
I'll be right here when you need a friend.

Everything means nothing,
when the past is just forgotten.
Something has to give.
I guess it might as well be me.
Within a broken dream,
where even shadows seem to scream.
You and I; we are not the same,
but I can't change.

Tonight, as your body resonates.
I can feel you call for me.
Close your eyes, there is no need to debate.
All your whispers will defeat.

Through the broken glass,
where every feeling starts to smash.
I will not be afraid.
Past the broken bridge,
where we used to play as kids.
I know you still feel the same,
but I can't change.

FRAGILITY

For you, my queen, are an offering.

But from which side I am not yet sure.

Have you been sent from the heavens to show me the euphoric ambience of true love's kiss?

A lifetime of warm radiance and afterglow easing me into the shadows,

like a fireplace and a bottle of vino entombed in a chalet as a cold winter's snow storm blows outside?

Or;

Have you been delivered from darker places, to test my patience and virtue? How far I will go and how black I will let my insides turn waiting for the circle of our unity to reform?

Or;

Are you a mixture of both?

THE BATTLE OF LOLA MAYNE

I can feel the ties that bind us unravel, my love.
Like the death of a falling star fading back into the darkness.
The end of this euphoric whirlwind.
The end of this manic rollercoaster.
Just remember,
as we stand defeated,
in hope that time heals all wounds;
You have consumed far too much of my heart to ever let you go.
There isn't enough time left within this life,
or the next,
to heal and forget.

You are always a part of me.
I am always with you.

FRAGILITY

Through the unravelling veil of our decaying temple,
the thorns all beam and glisten;
As if portraying razor wire,
lining the walls we had built around ourselves.
And although these walls kept us safe,
they also kept us trapped within.
We allowed ourselves to smile,
but forfeit the feeling of true happiness.

There were times when it felt as though we were getting back on track. But then something would ultimately reignite the fury once again, and surrender us both hurt, licking our wounds beyond the fallout.

Throughout the climactic events and unstable environment, barrages of discomforting conversations and arguments, I never fell out of love with Lola. My heart still yearned for her with the same intensity as the day we first met. I didn't blame her for our situation. This was a team effort.

We continue to move in these circles.
Some wide and full of anguish until we crash back into each other again,
like two waves becoming one as they reach the shore.
Some small and yet significant, just a break between what was, to what is, and then back to what was again.
And although these distances vary,
they somehow have a way of dimming the light inside each of our souls, and then reigniting them again, instantaneously.
Yet we still end up at the same conclusion.
Although these circles seem to get us nowhere,
possibly they are trying to reveal what is supposed to be.

I have watched as you have lowered and raised your walls like a boom gate to the chambers of your soul.

When you let me inside, I see beauty, a flourishing garden that begs to creep out into the streets and cover over your stone entombed heart. I see magic that even the greatest illusionist would envy.

I see truth.

I see desire.

I see pure happiness.

But then, when it looks as though you are finally able to release yourself from this handmade cage;

The walls go up again.

The boom gates close.

And I wait patiently for them to rise again.

FRAGILITY

And I am forced to think;
Where does one's mind wander when the world gets her down?
Are there circuits in her thoughts so deep and dark that even I cannot shine light upon them in times like these?
Is the warmth of my touch not enough to tear apart the skies and let the sun shine down whatever black shaded streets she walks down within her head?
Do my words disintegrate at the walls she has risen?
How can anything veer her away from remembering the beautiful soul that she is?
What secrets and subconscious collectives can take an angel and cast her into hell?
For before this day the only tears that I had witnessed were the ones that came with laughter.
But these tears;
These tears have shades of venomous darkness.
These tears do not come bearing a smile.

Often,
the antidote is within the poison.
This thing that is killing us,
also has the power to bring us back to life.
Shed away the skin of false starts.
Peel back the surface and dissect the feelings within.
For we have both found what we were ultimately searching for.
A fire that we cannot control.
Pull apart the blinds and let the light pierce this darkness.
Leave not a shadow for the hurt to hide.
As in this light,
gods and goddesses walk among us.
Let them watch us shine.
A king and his queen.
A queen and her king.
Eventually this empire will rise,
And we will walk,
untouchable.

Together.

FRAGILITY

The debris from our fire,
cascades in the wind.
The ashes of time burnt away.
If either chooses not to stoke the embers,
then this difficulty surely falls on the other.
If neither chooses to stoke the embers,
then the flames,
and everything they stand for,
are destined to die.

It had been so long since we had retreated from the city. Years, even. Every day had become the same as the one prior, and the one to follow, as we focused on our careers to try to cloak the thought of our then disintegrating marriage.

After one of our then-weekly arguments, Lola suggested we disappear to the country for a week or two in order to try and rekindle our flame. Just the notion alone reinstated to me that she still cared enough to try, and with that, we were organising our trip to refresh.

FRAGILITY

For it is here,
in the fragments of peril we stand.
My hand in yours,
and neither of us wanting to say goodbye.
But moving forward has tired us both.
So we wait;
For a resolution.
For a miracle.
We wait.
Our binds are far too strong to break,
and our hearts;
Still beat as one.
I am still on your side.
I am still your biggest fan.

Magnetic affiliation consumes me.
The name that tangles my tongue and renders my throat dry;
Packaged prison as a privilege.
I sit in wait as the storm grows dark.
Holding onto faith that it cannot rain forever.
So suspend me in your tangled heart,
for eternity continues to whisper your name.
And although the radiating light from each heartbeat dims,
there is still enough glow to light the fire again.

FRAGILITY

All of these hurdles,
all of these hoops.
To try to deny,
ourselves of the truth.
To push far away,
when we want to pull close.
To not say the things,
that we need to say most.
To soften the burn,
by not saying your name.
To not see your face.
To not feel this pain.

I sat on the back porch of our hired country retreat. Drawing back on a cigarette, I could still hear Lola weeping through an open window above me.

This had gone the exact opposite direction than either of us were anticipating. Right there, the thought finally dawned upon me;

'Would Lola be happier without me?'

Was my endurance of affection toward her really only entrapment to consume my own selfish wants and desires, energised by my own need for love? My wanting for things to revert back to the way that they were to cradle my own personal aspirations? My dreams?

Ultimately, would Lola recapture true happiness upon my embarkation?

At the peak of my unapologetic tirade an epiphany occurred.
Was my quest to make her happier really just destroying her instead?
Although I wanted the best for her,
Was the best for her my non existence in her life?
I try with all my might to pull away,
To leave her be;
To just give up.
But letting go of her would be letting go of the greatest parts of myself.

Are the stars falling in reverse?
Have we met the peak of this mountain,
or, have we somehow lost our way through the spiralling paths and rocky formations?
Am I still your one?
Do our hearts still beat in unison?
Can you feel me when I'm not there?
Or, am I alone?

FRAGILITY

The feeling of these jagged nails clawing at me does not get any easier.
As I wait for you in the forgotten corners of this cold dark shell.
Just to hear your voice,
or to feel your touch.
I will not beg you,
or plead you,
to say the things I long to hear you say.
And as I sift through these ashes of time burnt up;
Time we could be nestled within open fields of flowers.
Yellow and violet.
Violent,
vibrance.
I conjure up hope,
knowing that you too are suffering in your own cell you cannot retreat from.
All the while;
The answers,
However blurred,
linger within us.

THE BATTLE OF LOLA MAYNE

I can see your struggle,
my queen.
And believe me,
it casts the shades and turns my insides as black as your own.
My thoughts as dark and restless as yours.
For we both lay helpless;
And although I hold you as tight as I possibly can as sadness crawls from your eyes;
And although I feed you my warmth, trying to recharge you in your darkest of hours,
this room is still cold.
These thoughts are still tarnished.
This light is still fading.

FRAGILITY

If I have to forfeit my dreams in order for your happiness,
then so it will be.
I will still belong to you.
My every heartbeat will still scream your name,
and my longing will continue far after your mouth has forgotten
 how to speak my name.
But your happiness,
that is what is truly important here;
It always has been.

THE BATTLE OF LOLA MAYNE

I'm sick of crying,
I'm sick of trying,
and absolutely nothing is the way that it should be!

Things falling apart are not always recognisable. Sometimes, while you ponder your situation, it is happening within the background.

Often it happens so incoherently that by the time you realise, it is far too late.

I will never forget Lola locking herself in the bathroom and pleading me to leave as I stood frozen on the opposite side of the door. It derived from an argument not uncommon to us, although this particular time, ultimately fatal to our union.

To this day I wish I never followed her order to leave. For by the time I returned to the apartment, Lola was gone, placing a bullet between my teeth, and swinging a hammer toward it with all of her might.

The death of us was the spiritual death of myself.

THE BATTLE OF LOLA MAYNE

Not fire nor flood could ever stop me.
From wanting.
From waiting.
From believing.
Because true faith does not set time limits.
True feelings do not crash like waves and disintegrate atop the shore.
True love is nothing short of eternal.
And as my body yearns in decay,
for your warmth.
For your touch;
The door will always be ajar,
Awaiting your return.
So please,
I beg of you;
Take from me this ball of flesh.
Place it delicately on sticks and straw.
Cast the very same match you first used to ignite us;

And burn,

my heart,

to ashes.

CHAPTER FOUR
FRACTURE

And now, her heart is not mine;

Much as the moon, or the stars, or the glistening light across the first waves break as the sun presents itself to the morning skies.

This new day is not bright.

There is no sun.

There is no light.

Just a dark overcast of thunder clouds,

breaking,

as I,

to release this powerful energy within.

I reach for my phone and where her name would appear and light up my world like a million Christmas lights scattered as far as the eye could see,

All that is left is her beautiful face beneath a cracked screen.

And the time.

And what does time even mean now?

For the time we had was the only time that mattered.

The rest is but a waste.

A yearning want for her to be back within my arms like an egg nestled within its nest.

What do I do with all of this dead time?

And if you cannot be mine,
Then whose will you be?
Will he long for you the way I've longed?
Will he beg for you the way I've begged?
Will he drop down to both knees in the middle of a storm, rain flooding down like a million tears from above;
And confess his absolution to you?
Or will he scar you?
Will he make you wish you never left?
Will he make you want to be back home;
Here.
With me.
I could not stop you from leaving,
And if setting you free is what I needed to do,
then I will bear the cross for both of us.
But I could never deny you.
I will always be an open door.
For you are my one true love.
And if this leaves me bitter and twisted and unable to go on with anybody else;
Then at the least,
I know that it was real.

FRACTURE

Tear us apart.
We detonate.
You had my heart.
But threw it away.
Tear us apart.
We detonate.
I self-destruct.
You fade away.

People rarely give you forewarning of what happens when relationships fail. They illuminate the sanction of marriage, and they encourage you to 'make decisions that are right for you', but nobody actually has the answers to combat the despair that comes after separation. I could feel my heart grow tight, even breathing was becoming a challenge. I couldn't eat. I couldn't sleep. I would just lay there staring at the ceiling, thinking of her.

I was still very much in love with Lola. There was absolutely no denying that. She was the most captivating person I had ever met. She still is.

I had not known the exact meaning of true love before her arrival, and as I prayed that this would end, and convinced myself that we would eventually get back together, I did not realise that everyone else in my life had fallen wayside, and I was truly alone.

FRACTURE

It was three am,
And I was thinking of you.
Again.
Still.
I used to really enjoy being in bed,
With you.
But now instead of your arms draped over me as we sleep,
Or your nails carving scratches down my back,
I lay awake as your absence tears me apart.
There are days that my body aches for you,
And the yearning is almost too much to bear.
The sound of your name as it passes through my lips sends electricity on fire through my veins.
Maybe we weren't supposed to be forever.
And maybe you weren't supposed to stay.
But the longer you're away,
And the further out of reach you get;
The more the static of this emptiness grows.

These idle hands that beckon your touch.
These withered uncalculated words that burst to break free from
　　one's quivering lips.
Angelic dialect,
entombed within the fragility of rice paper confinement.
The warm glow of salvation shadowing upon its surface.
Rupturing light throughout the most familiar of places.
Expel me of this treacherous void.
Consume me so I can rise like the phoenix,
and bask in the radiating aura of your love.

FRACTURE

Somewhere on the outskirts of time we lay.
My fingers crawling through your hair while the other hand traces spirals on your skin.
Our souls unravelled yet somehow still entwined.
For your touch is the antidote I seek.
For lonely nights,
and waves of fire that roll inside of me.
A burning I cannot extinguish.
The warm afterglow of a place I've not yet forgotten,
and throughout the famine of our love,
never will.
For it is when our two worlds collide that we are truly whole.
So, I will wait right here,
Feet firmly planted where you left me.
And even if vines grow around these legs,
and tighten their grip around this hollow shell,
this is where I will be.
This is where you will find me.

THE BATTLE OF LOLA MAYNE

I've tried to wipe my hands,
tell myself I'll start again.
But the ink of you has bleed right through.
Through my bones.
My heart.
My soul.
So there is no way,
that I could ever get you off of me.
The memories,
or what you mean to me.
I could not even begin to tell you how many times I've stroked my fingers across your face through this screen.
How many nights I've let tears blur my vision until just the illuminating glow is all that was left.
I tried tirelessly to delete our memories all the way to the bottom of a thousand empty bottles,
but yet they still remained.
As your side of the bed still remains empty.
There isn't a human in this world that could ever replace you there.
So why even bother trying?

FRACTURE

Darkness unfolding,
The light begins to shine.
Inside I'm still holding,
a place where I can hide.
I wander within armies,
out into the world.
In hope that,
I find what,
I've been searching for.

I remember the nights,
Where we moved like clockwork.
Our heartbeats seconds,
That warm embrace minutes,
That raging fire hours.
And although we still tick on,
universally.
Our time together,
is now time apart.
I'll wait for you on the other side.

The never ending pattern of ruminating thought was tearing me apart. I couldn't go a single minute without clusters of memories and time spent together forming within my mind. I would lay in bed at night, exhausted, but every time I closed my eyes all I could see was her.

I tried every self help therapy option I could get my hands on. Hypnosis, calming music of storms and Native American flutes with war drums and wolves howling in the background; but nothing seemed to work. Finally, I succumbed to seeing a doctor. He prescribed me Valium and sent me on my way. I will never forget the bittersweet feeling that night of laying in bed, and finally, watching Lola's face fade.

THE BATTLE OF LOLA MAYNE

If love was a story,
made to make us grow.
Then these chapters have ended,
and this book has been closed.
I sit all alone now,
I can't leave this house.
I know you don't want me,
I blame myself.
I hear that you've moved on,
I don't know what to do.
We've been through some good times,
but there were bad times too.
I can't stop this shaking,
I don't sleep at night.
I'm gradually breaking,
I hear you're alright.

I just want to touch you.
I just want to hold onto you.
I just want to feel you.
Next to me.

FRACTURE

Inside my hollow heart,
I've felt this feeling from the start.
Didn't you say we could be something?
You have me so confused,
I don't know what I should do,
now that you tell me this means nothing.

Sometimes life doesn't go as planned.
Turn the tables - take me off my feet again.
And I held the whole world in my hands.
I feel so deceived,
I can't believe,
in anything.

I wish that we could stay.
Together.
Forever.
When you left it went so grey.
Inside of you.
Inside of me.
Where did you go?
Why did you leave?
Abandoned me.
Didn't you say that we could be
Something?

I wish I could see you smile.
I wish I could call you up,
make things alright.
It's burning me inside.
I will try not to cry,
when we reunite.
And to my sweetest friend.
Good times should never end.
Will you be waiting?
Waiting for me?
When the skies have opened up,
will we seek for each other?
Will it be the same?
Good times should never end.

FRACTURE

Like the imaginative excellence of a little boy's dreams, that traffic lights are controlled by mice on a mission; the mind can lead you down alleyways filled with naivety, based on pure hope, that everything in this world is possible.
But after conclusive patterned thought it seems that this is not always the case,
and sometimes the mice turn out to be more systematic impulse.

And with this epiphany,
I will rebuild the walls.

This shouldn't take long.

Awakening from my favourite dream.
I remember you oh so well.
Like a goddess from above,
gazing down upon a lion lapping at the water's edge.
The look in his eyes carving scratches into your soul as the humidity rises.
Animalistic impulses at catastrophic levels surging through us.
A collaboration of hearts.
Flesh on flesh.
Fire on fire.

FRACTURE

And the sky goes black.
The whole world goes numb.
And the book slams shut.
All the doors just close.
And I can't move forward.
Yet I can't turn back.
I can feel myself breaking.
And the blood run black.
But the memory still holds.
Every crevice of your skin.
Every smile in the doorway.
Every thought trapped within.

As I walked to the corner shop to buy cigarettes, I saw Lola walking toward me. She was just metres ahead before she looked up and locked eyes with mine. I could see the shock cast on her face; this was the first time we had seen each other since the end of our relationship.

Lola looked perfect, as always, and I guess by this stage I was a little more bedraggled.

I'm not sure if it was the sleepless nights, or the fact that I hadn't eaten properly in months; Unkempt hair, steadily increased drinking habit or my then newly settled prescription addiction, but it's safe to say I was not looking my best.

She smiled, what appeared nervously, and asked how I had been.

We traded pleasantries and within minutes our interaction was over.

This chance meeting, as brief as it was, only added fuel to the already rapidly growing downward spiral.

FRACTURE

Set me on fire one last time.
But this time, be sure I am burnt to ashes.
Leave no trace of body or embers.
Let the tiny flakes blow away into the breeze,
until there is absolutely nothing left of me.
No heart to beat your name.
No soul to entwine with your own.
Just a vacant mass of flesh and bone.
Glazed over eyes where perfection once reflected.

Set me on fire.
One last time.
And as you walk away,
remember.

What you meant to me.

What I meant to you.

THE BATTLE OF LOLA MAYNE

Your eyes,
they scream at me.
Inside,
I'm cold and grey.
Tonight,
I give to you.
My heart,
and whole life through.
I watched,
as you took the step.
And now,
I have nothing left.
Your faith,
is so disguised.
Now I,
am hypnotised.
The fire,
it burnt so bright.
That I,
faded to the light.
One wish,
one hope,
one day.
I know,
I am not OK.

You can tear me down.

CHAPTER FIVE
EMOTION SICKNESS

EMOTION SICKNESS

When all is said and done,
and you're left on your own,
will you be afraid?
When the streets don't seem so safe,
and your heart's an empty place,
will you be afraid?

When you're lost inside yourself,
and my picture's off your shelf,
will you feel the same?
When it's burning to the core,
and you can't take any more,
will you feel the same?

When you scratch your feelings bare,
and nobody seems to care,
will you think of me?
When you're screaming in yourself,
and nobody hears a sound,
then will you believe?

THE BATTLE OF LOLA MAYNE

Allow me to paint you a picture,
some of the things that I'm sure you would have missed.
Nights where I dropped down to my knees,
and prayed to a god I now don't believe exists.
And you were probably warm and cozy,
in the arms of somebody else.
While I sat there cold and lonely,
drinking away the best parts of myself.
While in the pit of my stomach,
I felt the embers still crackle and burn.
As demons whom walk on water,
and then claim themselves as saints,
were grinning from horn to twisted horn;
while they clicked the tips of their decaying hoofnails and basked in what they had created.
And as they reached down and struck me with their unfathomable vengeance for a fairytale left unfinished.
Through monsoons of black sea serpents tearing at the twisted pieces of what was left.
In the sinking desperation to recapture what we were,
what we are,
and what we could have ultimately been;
I still wouldn't have changed a thing.

EMOTION SICKNESS

You must have gotten amnesia!
You must have forgotten everything that we once were!
Do you even recall the lion's den?
The piercing look from across the room?
The flick of a forked tongue?
The gnawing at each other's soul?
The grip that left you gasping for air?
The heart?
The fire?
The passion?
There is not a single part of me that will allow myself to believe
   that you have forgotten.
What we are.
What we were.
Two stars crashing into one another,
both born from universes light years away,
yet destined to collide.

There are certain things that we as humans do, that we do not wish to admit, when it comes to ex-partners and social media. For the record, it had been a long while since I had 'checked up' on Lola's homepage, although I do recall that one particular analysis was definitely more detrimental than the rest.

Upon noticing a change in her relationship status, that up until this point had read single, I recall the feeling of every single imperceptible cell within my body combust, as the true game of self-loathing and decay had yet to truly hit its peak.

EMOTION SICKNESS

I'm glad that you are happy now.
And the memory of what we were has passed.
I'm glad you can smile,
and be content,
forgetting us.
I'm glad you no longer see my face,
when you close your eyes,
as I do yours.
And I'm glad you have found someone.
To erase.
Me.

I am the moth that circles the campfire at night.
So close that it burns, but yet still captivated by the light.
And the darkness around it, I too can feel, but dare not enter.
   For I have felt those feelings before, and would rather burn.
And if the lover for whom I burn can no longer accept me for
   who I am, then, reject me for who I am!
I will crawl deep into the numbness of this cocoon, and resurrect
   like Jesus Christ.
With god like status I will return, and the emptiness within my
   vacant shell will remain frozen in the past.
Frozen in time.
Until my sun does not shine.
And these words they bounce like cannonballs in my head.
Because not all wars are fought on battlefields.
And not all wars have a beginning,
or the beginning of an end.
And no war is simple.
Especially,
When it's a war within yourself.

EMOTION SICKNESS

Alone as,
I feel the systems break inside myself.
I know that,
It won't be long before they aren't sent for help.
In my room,
I see the pictures,
memories,
near and far.
Pills and tubes,
they try to mark down one more day before I...

Deep inside,
I feel it burning faster every single day.
I'm not angry,
just overcome with all that could have been.
This sickness,
it's getting far too much for me to take.

There is no escape.

From this cancer.

This constant battle within myself.
Can I keep this up forever?
My heart begs me to let go of this tyrannical tantrum,
this war within myself.
My body yearns,
as my soul wipes the tears from its own illuminating cheeks,
constantly forcing itself to recompose.
Yes, it is true;
The walls I have built,
with the blood and tears of memories that haunt,
have kept them all out.
But they have also trapped me in.
So now,
I suffocate in this space that I had formerly built to heal.

EMOTION SICKNESS

Clouds in your head.
Will always form.
While you are scared.
You don't belong.
You hold this life.
In your two hands.
You can't give up.
You can't pretend.
Fake smiles show.
How hurt you are.
You cannot grow.
Without a past.
I'm in your head.
Deep in your veins.
I hide the hurt.
And kill the pain.

It was becoming an all too familiar occurrence that my inner nostril became clogged, and the tiny white flakes would just fall from my nose, showering back onto the plate. The dark circles that were ever present below my eyes and the pasty beige drug nectar that collected at the corners of my mouth between lacklustre cracked lips had been present far longer than I would prefer to admit.

Upon reflection, this was it. I had finally reached my conclusive destination. This was rock bottom. But at the time, I was far too fucked up to realise it.

Standing in a poorly lit bathroom,
my former child self echoing back at me from the ridged surface of a blood cracked mirror.
The smile on his face;
Wonder in his eyes.
Unknowing of how the world is eventually going to chew him up, and spit him back out again.
Unknowing of how broken he will eventually become.
What lessons can I teach him?
Or,
reflective,
what lessons can he teach me?
I reach out to grab for his hand but my footing slips and he turns away.

Oh, the places you will go.

Ever so often,
I can still see the shadow of dying butterfly wings batting against the inside of my chest.
I feel as they exhaustedly try to stretch their wings and reach out of this cage with the limited energy that they have left.
But as the light starts to dim inside,
I can see that even they are losing hope,
of ever getting back to you.

These bugs all feel like atom bombs,
they crawl in my ears and through my nose,
but I don't have the energy to stop them.
For they all have their demons too,
that burn inside,
and reproduce,
and nothing that I do or say can help them.
Their eyes all shine like dynamite,
they kick and scream,
thrash and fight,
the darkness they're creating is never ending.
And every little step I take,
I end right back at my mistakes,
and no one in this god damn world can help me.

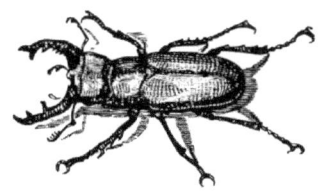

THE BATTLE OF LOLA MAYNE

I've got no religion.
I've got no control.
I've got no ambition.
Life's so complicated now.
I've got no more theories,
about the way I feel.
I tried to stuff it all inside,
but it just piled up again.
I've got nothing left to give,
and there ain't nothing left to take.
I'm a worthless piece of shit.
I'm a dirty big mistake.
I can end this torture now,
but I can't stop this fucking pain.
I just want to close my eyes,
And never open them again.

Big machines,
with horns and wings.
Stab inside,
but can't break free.
When the sickness comes,
I'm the only one.
Why can't you see,

this is killing me.

EMOTION SICKNESS

Put the pedal down a little harder.
Make this system go a little faster.
In and out back into lane again.
Take another hit and let's begin.
Lights are flashing round and around the bends.
Just another wreckage on the brink.
Please standby don't try to stop me here.
I can push this piece of flesh to go harder than you think.

THE BATTLE OF LOLA MAYNE

Six Valium, a gram of Cocaine, eight beers, half a Xanax, two Percocet, a bottle of Jack Daniels, three points of Meth, four lines of Speed, a taste of Ketamine, and finally, one tiny bump of Fentanyl, to make my entire house of cards come crashing down.

They say that when you die you see a bright beaming light and angels come down from heaven to carry you home. I personally can conclude that this is not, in fact, the truth. As in with my experience with death, it was far more similar to when you get dunked by a wave. Spinning frantically in the dark, fighting to reach the surface.

Unsurprisingly, the following three days I can only recall snippets of. Red and blue lights illuminating the darkness. Glaring fluorescence flashing by as I am pushed hurriedly into the emergency room, and a thin veiled blue curtain slowly being pulled shut as my weary eyes fell back into the darkness. This was my warning shot, my courtesy call, my opportunity to re-evaluate, everything.

Addicts' prayer:

Deliver me from all things that I can no longer recall.
Traps I have fallen into and time I have let slide through my hands.
Damaging pastimes and honed skills that just embody rituals I no longer wish to perform.
The razor that scrapes across the mirror,
chained to the rolled note.
Or the burnt-bottom spoon, awaiting the tip of my false idols.
Give me the power to forgive myself,
and the strength I need to start my new day afresh.
Do not save me,
but rather show me how to save myself.
For this is no longer fun.
This is no longer happiness.

Amen.

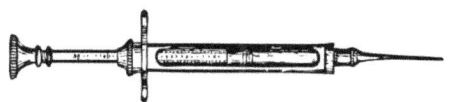

THE BATTLE OF LOLA MAYNE

I woke up today,
in the strangest place I'd ever been before.
I looked at my reflection in the mirror,
and couldn't see myself anymore.

All these years gone by.
Somebody else's memories inside my mind.
When did all things change?
Let me start again.

Nobody told me,
what I'd become.
Nobody showed me,
so I just run.

You think that the ones that you love would be enough,
but sometimes they're not.

The old me is ending.

And my life,

has just begun.

I am awakening.

EMOTION SICKNESS

It's too late
tonight.
To try to
reignite.
Opinions,
left to linger.
As the past falls,
through my fingers.

Somehow,
someway.
I'll find you,
someday.
The vicar
lights a candle.
For these thoughts that
I can't handle.

Holding
onto something.
I keep searching,
it keeps coming.
If I find it,
will I be glad?
Or is this all
that I have left?

THE BATTLE OF LOLA MAYNE

This fortress
of feeling.
Unspoken,
unhealing.
All these symptoms,
still persisting.
Weary eyes can't
keep resisting.

It's over,
I can feel it.
Through the searching,
I have healed it.
I don't care now,
memories scattered.
And these thoughts are
only phantoms.

EMOTION SICKNESS

Forgive me.
As I retreat.
To stitch these wounds.
And swab these scars.
In this time,
know.
I will return.
With fire in my blood;
And a rested heart.

CHAPTER SIX
ACCEPTANCE

ACCEPTANCE

The storm has subsided,
and with it,
taken everything.

My hopes and dreams,
wants and desires.

Now all that remains,
is the dirt.

A fresh start.

Each day I get a little bit stronger.
A little more resilient.
With each and every hand grenade that catapults toward my heart,
and explodes into a million pieces.
I gather the shards,
articulately place them back together.
And reconstruct.
I close my eyes.
Inhale.
Exhale.
And upon reopening them,
my faith is a little stronger than before.
A little more armoured.
And a little more ready for the next grenade.
The next wave to pull me under and throw me around like a rag doll.
I close my eyes.
Inhale.
Exhale.
And as I reopen them,
and fight against the tides,
she lingers by the water's edge.

ACCEPTANCE

And for a second there,
I thought I had found my place.
After all the searching,
and conquests.
The highest highs,
and lowest lows.
I finally felt free.
I finally felt,
Home.

It had been seven long, hard, sober months since what I now refer to as 'the incident'.

My health had greatly improved and was evident in my appearance. I no longer looked decayed, my skin no longer grey.

The people I had lost throughout my descent were slowly, but more responsively, starting to reach out as I regained their trust and acceptance, and began reconnecting to the world I once knew.

I had taken so many wrong turns post the separation of Lola and I, but I was doing everything within my power to continue my sobriety.

I vividly recall standing atop the water's edge. Sand between my toes, waves diminishing at my feet. The sun falling away behind the ocean's horizon, and a surfboard propped up against me.

Me... Attempting to surf...

Within this moment, I remember the sweeping feeling of absolute freedom. No obsessions. No addictions. Just myself and the waves.

A smile crept across my face as I celebrated my recovery.

ACCEPTANCE

Go free now,
the demons in my head.
Just sleep now,
tomorrow's almost here.
Come through me,
into the morning light.
Don't deny yourself,
to try to end the fight.
Don't destroy your dreams,
because the day is drawing close.
And something in the wind says,
things will change again.

There are always going to be parts of me that belong to you alone.
My arms,
that embraced you.
My heart,
that will eternally scream your name.
And,
of course,
the webbing between my left thumb and forefinger,
which steadies the pen,
to tell the world just how beautiful you are.

ACCEPTANCE

My mother once told me,
it's not always roses.
And it never meant much to me,
until, you came and cut them all down.
She said there would be days,
where the sounds are so sweet.
And sometimes we fall,
for the people we meet.
But then sometimes we fall,
in a different direction.
I didn't believe her then,
but that was a long, long time,
before I met you.

My mother once told me,
that life is a garden.
The more that you put in,
the more you're rewarded.
But if the sun doesn't shine,
or the rain doesn't come.
Then the work you've put in,
will just all turn to dust.
Yet I questioned her thought,
though I had no suggestion.
You taught me things,
that I guess I should have already known.

Upon the second glance;

Raindrops creeping silently down the windows of a West End coffee shop.
A disorientating feeling of déjà vu cast across me as she places her order and rummages through her handbag for loose change.
Thanking the barista, she gently tucks her hair behind her ear, before finally raising her eyes to meet mine.

'Hello Lola…'

Lola smiled, obviously acknowledging the improvements I'd made. I had a million things to say to her, but instead, let them all fall wayside in order for a fresh, new beginning.

She questioned me of my progress and in a heartfelt, empathetic manner, advocated how proud she was; making a brief comment on my glowing appearance.

Her coffee cup was practically empty by the time we said our goodbyes, hugging briefly, before gesturing to stay in contact.

As she walked away, I felt the embers flicker inside, but this time, I did not let them engulf me. Instead, I just smiled, and ordered my latte to go.

ACCEPTANCE

It began like the collision of two stars;
Complete darkness suddenly forming a light so bright it could steal the colour from your eyes.
Pixelated vision making even her silhouette difficult to make out.
But the aura transcended me far into territories unknown.
A light so bright that it could burn for eternity, given the chance.
But now, as the darkness of our kinship crawls back in,
And only the occasional shimmer of stardust flickers in my eyes.
I will always remember,
when our stars collided.

THE BATTLE OF LOLA MAYNE

There is always going to be that thing.
That thing that reminds me of how your eyes glimmer like the sun.
Or the way your lips rest,
slightly open,
as your beauty resonates across the room.
I will find you within songs,
within art,
within words.
I will see your face upon the most beautiful sculptures.
And hear your voice echo within the rumbles of thunder.
But mostly,
when the day turns to night,
and all the lights go out;
I will find you in the darkness.
I will feel your warmth surround me,
and remind me that I am not alone.
That no matter how far you are,
or how long it has been since I have heard your voice mutter my name,
you are still with me.

ACCEPTANCE

I will wait for you,
at the edge of the shadows.
Burning bright,
like the light from a candle.
Flickering through,
the winds of a hurricane.

One million miles away.

After completing my thirteenth month of sobriety my sponsor suggested I moved down to Houston to help her run a small support group of struggling alcoholics and reformed addicts. Leaving everything behind made me anxious, but I decided that ultimately, the change would serve me well.

I hadn't seen Lola since our encounter at the coffee shop, and for my own benefit, I planned to keep things that way. Admittedly, I missed her greatly, but Lola meant far too much to me for us to ever be 'just friends'. Any attempt to do so would only hinder my progress and potentially undo how far I had come.

ACCEPTANCE

I'm not beside you,
holding your hand or swirling my fingers across the small of your back.
I'm not directly in your eye sight, reassuring you of my presence in your life.
I'm not there for you to unload all of your frustrations upon.
But I am with you.
With every breath.
With every single step.
I'm in the whisper of the trees.
Within the light dancing across vacant faces as you captivate this new world.
Between the thoughts that transcend from one to another,
I am with you.

As you are with me.

THE BATTLE OF LOLA MAYNE

There is no love without pain.
Without truth and uncertainty.
Without knowing what you deserve;
And having the courage to reach out and take it.
In a fragile world where everything moves past so quickly,
where dramatic change unfurls in the blink of an eye;
Follow your instincts.
Follow the ever dying want to be accepted.
To be cherished.
To be appreciated.
For in these tiny crevasses of the heart's bleeding core;
Destiny resides,
hope lingers,
and true love blossoms.

ACCEPTANCE

Somewhere deep within the spiritual undercurrent,
the light of simmering ashes still flicker.
Although the flames have died down,
the embers of life lay in wait for their time to reignite.
Through buried passages of our transcending consciousness,
we are now as we will always be.

Whole.

There will be times that I am completely forgotten;
But the times that I am remembered are where whirlwinds will take the embers,
pushing them closer toward the surface.
Forcing a smile to cast across your face.
Illusive memories so vivid you can almost feel my arms wrapping their warmth around you.
In the times you need me most,
I will always remain here.

THE BATTLE OF LOLA MAYNE

The confusion has subsided.
The worry,
left to tremble under a million stars.
The Battle of Lola Mayne is not won,
nor lost.
But still.
Paused for an unspoken moment in time.
Five years?
Ten?
This lifetime?
That is not at all relevant.
As the souls are still entwined.
Two hearts still beat as one.
The rhythmic tide of our ocean still moves in unison.
And for now.
In this void.
I will work harder on me,
for her.

ACCEPTANCE

I love you.
I will always love you.
I don't need to be next to you,
or be inside of your arms,
as you will always be inside of mine.
Deep within my chest,
guiding me to absolution.
I will forever use the light of your love to show me the way home.
The everlasting flame.
The eternal melting heart.
You are my everything.

Until we meet again.

Always.

THE BATTLE OF LOLA MAYNE

It's a rather peculiar situation, praying for someone's return, whilst also actively trying to avoid them. To say that I had forgotten my undying devotion toward Lola, or had completely given up on us ever rekindling what we had, would be a complete and utter lie. (As crazy and unrealistic as that statement may seem, given the situation.) I still maintain faith that fate works in mysterious ways and what is meant to be, will eventually be. This person, who had come into my life and single handedly resurrected who I was, who tapped into my innermost sanctums and showed me the true meaning of unconditional love, would forever hold the greater parts of my heart. And although I will not seek for her, I am open to be found.

I do, however, no longer let our distance consume me. Instead, whenever she crosses my mind, I just smile and wish for her happiness.

And while my fire still burns bright for her, as I assume it always will; I have learnt that sometimes letting the person you value the most go, in order to maintain their happiness, is one of the greatest sacrifices you could possibly ever make.

I wish herself, and her partner, all the very best...

ACCEPTANCE

I have learnt,
to embrace the climactic events of life.
To not live in the future,
nor in the past.
But within this exact moment.
To be 100% true to myself,
regardless of how others feel about it.
To be content in my loneliness,
and captivated by the crowds.
I have learnt that true happiness is a state of mind,
and sometimes;

Love is real.

AUTHOR'S NOTES

Dear reader,

The love, affection, and all other emotive responses written within these pages are entirely up to your own interpretation. What some may see as romanticism, others may find unhealthy and obsessive.

If you do however find that your current personal circumstance resonates with the mid to latter sections of the book, please know that you are not alone, and help is always available.

While I have this opportunity, I would like to thank Ander Louis, for the frustrating task of advising on this piece, to the point of banning me from using 'lists of adjectives', and pushing me to write better, sharper, greater. This wouldn't have been what it is without your efforts, so thank you.

My beautiful Family, which have had to endure my often 'not so cautious' life decisions, but always continue to give me a reason to smile and try harder. I love you all more than you could ever imagine.

Teneille 'Gypsy' Mancarella, for her ongoing (usually blunt, but always honest) support in achieving any of this. You are an absolute godsend and the best friend anyone could ever ask for.

StephKat, Peta Page, Dean Mc, Jodie Douglas, Nikki Harris, Pete Walstab, Lauren X, and the entirety of my friends and family who have supported me throughout this journey. The life, as well as the art.

Thank you.

For the record, it was not all in vain.

As always, I would love to hear your feedback. Likes, dislikes, interpretations, theories and what resonated mostly with you.

Feel free to drop me a message on Facebook or Instagram @fallblind_

We all have our battles, Be kind to one another;

Always,

R. D. Rentmeester

www.ingramcontent.com/pod-product-compliance
Lightning Source LLC
Chambersburg PA
CBHW070257010526
44107CB00056B/2487